Her Father's Daughter

Letters From Love

Seun Omoha

Scribal Publishing
London

Dedication:

To the Father of fathers,
The one who calls me by name.

To the one who has given me
The tongue of the learned
To sustain with a word
Her who is weary.

To the I AM,
For the I AM,
Always.

Welcome Dear Sister

I'll let you in on a secret, these words were written for HIM.

Over many years, I journaled prayers and reflections across seasons of life. As time went on the nudge to share them with you came and many moons later, I am now obeying that nudge.

Seasons differ. Sometimes they are joyful, and our hearts overflow with gratitude. In other seasons, we need the Lord's surgical help to deal with the issues we see in our hearts.

Yet there are times when our strength seems weak, and we need frequent encouragement to regain the right perspective. And times when hope deferred makes the heart sick[i] and we must encourage ourselves in the Lord. Other times, we enter seasons of service where the object of our focus must be the Lord himself if we are to succeed at the assignment before us. Further, there are times when the upheaval of change requires us to seek an anchor for our soul to see us through.

In all these seasons, communion with the Lord is essential and the writings within this volume chronicle these precious dialogues. I welcome you to share in my *Book of Prayers, Thoughts and Quiet Studies* with my dearest Father. As you read, reflect on, and pray the words therein, it is my sincere prayer that you will find yourself in communion with the Lord.

I encourage you to look at the concluding section, The Spirit Walk on Emotions Avenue, which contains a glossary mapped against common emotions we face and a useful scripture reference to address each emotion. I hope you will find it handy as an alternative way to navigate the writings within this book.

If you are impacted by anything in this book, I would love to hear from you to learn how you too have overcome in the various seasons of life. Do reach out to me using the details below. I welcome an opportunity to share in your testimony.

Finally, watch out for the companion journal for Her Father's Daughter which will help you build your collection of prayers and reflection, your strategy for a spirit-guided life as you navigate various seasons of the soul.

The journey doesn't end here! To continue receiving inspiring prayers, reflections, scripture-based insights, doses of encouragement and updates on future releases - like the companion journal for Her Father's Daughter— simply click the link below to subscribe to my newsletter and let's stay connected as we grow in communion with Him together.

Subscribe today and be the first to hear about exciting new resources!

Copy and paste the link below to the browser of your choice to subscribe: https://tinyurl.com/hfd-devo.

Let us now dive together into these Letters from LOVE.

Seun Omoba,
August 2024
hfd.devotional@gmail.com

CONTENTS

Glorious things of you are spoken, O city of God... for the Most High himself will establish her.

Psalm 87: 3,5 (ESV)

SEUN OMOHA

Seasons of Gratitude

My Life finds its definition in you Lord

1. A GRATEFUL HEART

Father, I love you.
Thank you for your faithfulness to me,
Thank you for not leaving me in the miry clay,
Thank you for delivering me completely,
Thank you for your goodness to me.

You have filled my life with many good things,
Thank you for your kindness to me,
You show me mercy I don't deserve,
You forgave my sins, you died for me,
You live and you fight for me.

Thank you for the gift of your strength.
I don't know how I survived the past seasons,
But Lord, you made a way,
You sent me help,
For this, I give you thanks.

Thank you for the gift of protection,
Indeed, you are able to protect.
Thank you for sound health,
Thank you for your victory always.

Thank you for your divine favour,
Thank you for your godly wisdom,
I do not take for granted,
Your love and acts for me,
I am deeply thankful.

2. YOU THRILL MY HEART

Thank you, Daddy.

From the bottom of my heart,
To the depths of my soul,
I give you Praise.

You are worthy of my thanks,
You are faithful, my King,
The orchestrator of all,
My peace,
The lover of my soul.

Your favour astonishes me,
This manifestation of your greatness.

I humbly come,
A daughter in awe,
To your throne of grace,
To say thank you, Daddy.

Your faithfulness is forevermore,
Thank you for the privilege,
To experience your wonderful ways,
Every accolade received,
I present back to you,
The glory is yours,
The gratitude mine,
To adorn you with.

You thrill my heart, Lord,
Beyond what I express,
From within me today,
I pour my love on you.

Thank you, Daddy,
Great is your faithfulness.

3. HE WATCHES OVER

Lord, I come,
With a heart of gratitude,
Thank you for your steadfast love.

Thank you for being the one,
Who neither sleeps nor slumbers,[ii]
Thank you for watching over me.

You are faithful,
You are merciful,
You are able to keep,
All committed into your hands.

I am thankful, Daddy.

Glory to your name.

4. MANY REASONS

Lord, I have many reasons to be thankful.
Bless the Lord oh my soul and forget not his benefits.

Thank you for Life, the breath I breathe unassisted,
Thank you that I am well, spirit, soul & body,
Thank you for my mind, emotions, body, all parts of me,
Thank you for your perfect health.

Thank you for blessing the works of my hands,
Thank you for open doors, Thank you for divine provision.

Thank you for saving me, being with me, revealing yourself to me,
Thank you for your deliverance,
Thank you for your encouragement and correction,
Thank you for your power at work in and for me,
Thank you for building me up.

Thank you for everything you have deposited within me,
Thank you for not allowing me to be consumed by ill will and
ungodly schemes,
Thank you for showing yourself strong always,
Thank you for never leaving me.

Thank you for listening always,
Thank you for helping me,
You are worthy of my thanks.
Be glorified forevermore.

5. THE ONE I LOVE

Father, I thank you for your victory.

Thank you for uprooting every seed,
You have not planted,
For arising, taking victorious control,
Showing your power,
On my behalf.

Thank you for purifying my desire,
For being my stone of help,
For the blood of Jesus,
Shed for my victory.

Thank you, Holy Spirit,
For never leaving me,
Without a witness,
Of God's power at work.

6. A NEW THING

Thank you, Lord,
For new opportunities.

Opportunities for growth,
Advancement, building strength,
Moulding godliness in my inner being.

Strengthen me by your Holy Spirit,
Moment by moment.

That I gain the ability,
To maximise every opportunity,
You have placed before me.

Amen.

7. LORD OVER THE MOUNTAINS

You are Lord over the mountains,
You are Lord over the seas,
You are Lord over the Land,
You are Lord over the deep.

That's why I praise you, Holy One,

He who cares for the mountains,
Will surely care for me,
He who cares for the seas,
Will surely care for me.

That's why I praise you, Holy God.

He who cares for the land,
Will surely care for me,
The One from whom deep places daren't hide,
Will surely care for me.

That's why I praise you, Holy One,

To the One who sees me,
The One who cares for me,
The Holy One,
The Holy God,
I offer my praise.

8. YEARS END

As the year draws to a close,
I come before you, I stop,
I remember, and I thank you.

Thank you for strength,
For divine protection,
For joy and celebrations,
For divine provision at every turn.

Thank you for your continued faithfulness,
For journey mercies, For new territories,
For favour unparalleled.

Thank you for the new revelations,
For your presence and love,
For great wisdom,
For mercy, time and again.

Thank you for the bonds of love and family,
For my home,
For seeking out the lonely,
For placing us in families.

Thank you for life,
For health and wealth,
For sustaining grace,
For your friendship.

Thank you for your tender loving care,
For my spirit, soul, and body,
For all that concerns me,
For your purpose for my life.

For all these and more,
I give you thanks.

Seasons of the Heart

She treasured all these in her heart, she believed in God who can do all to fulfil his plans, for his glory.

9. A PURE HEART

Lord, on this day I pray for a purification of my life.

Purify my heart and motives,
My thoughts and speech,
My actions, attitude and character,
Purify every aspect of my life.

Blessed are the pure in heart, for they shall see God,[iii]
Blessed is the prepared womb, for it shall receive the pure seed.

Lord, I have been dancing around with impurity,
Even in my subconscious,
Please help me.

Uproot the wrong trees,
Leave standing only what is of you,
Every seed of anger, malice, manipulation,
Depression, discouragement, discord,
Pride, self-importance, lack of empathy, impatience,
Procrastination, overlooking things of value, lack of discernment,
Fear, lack of courage, overcompensation,
I lift to your surgical scrutiny.

All these are scales,
Inhibitions to the full flow of God in my life,
Purge such wrongful seeds from my person,
I do not want to be hindered,
From being who you have called me to be,
I want to function in every place you formed me to fill,

I do not want to be the carrier of a still-born purpose,
I want to fulfil the destiny you proclaimed over me,
When you thought of and made me.

10. A RIGHT SPIRIT

Lord, I have missed it,
I come to you for mercy,
I come to you for help,
You who decide where mercy is dispensed,
Favour me with your mercy,
Take my hand and lead me in the right direction.

I repent of wrongful attitudes,
I have allowed creep into my life,
I renounce them today,
I pray for grace to live out,
The fruit of the Holy Spirit.

The mirror of your word,
Shows my heart to me,
Almighty, cleanse me,
With your word and your blood,
Remove the stains,
Make me clean again,
Help me live from redemption.

Create in me a clean heart,[iv]
A pure heart,
A tender heart,
Responsive to you.

Cast me not away from your presence oh God,
Draw me close, pray for me, intercede for me,
Cover me under the shadow of your wings,
Let your flame be sustained in me,
By the oil of your Holy Spirit,
Until I become,
A full-blown flame.

Take not your Holy Spirit from me,
In myself, I am not wise,

I have no discernment,
I am not able to live,
A life pleasing to God,
It is you who pushes me,
Corrects and comforts me,
How I need you, Holy Spirit.

Take not your Holy Spirit from me,
It is you who helps me, intercedes for me,
And prays the will of the Father over me,
It is you that hovers over my life,
Filling every space,
Making the atmosphere of my life,
Conducive for the word of God to be fulfilled,
Holy Spirit, please don't ever leave me.

Restore unto me the joy of your salvation,
The fullness of what Jesus died to give me,
May I never despise that victory,
May I never despise that joy,
As each day unfolds,
Let me find,
Sweetness and satisfaction in you.

Renew a right spirit within me,
A spirit in constant communion with your Spirit,
A spirit nourished and fed to health,
In your goodness and guidance,
In malnourished areas,
I pray for divine sustaining food,
Propagating to a balanced diet,
All my days.

I pray all these,
In the name of the Father,
In the name of the Son, Jesus,
In the name of the Holy Spirit.
Amen.

11. UNAFRAID

Lord, I ask for the grace,
To serve you, In spirit and truth,
With integrity and sincerity.

I pray for cleansing,
So I boldly use,
All you've given me,
For your glory.

Cleanse my hands oh God,
Cleanse my mind.
Cleanse my heart oh God,
Cleanse my thoughts.

Cleanse my life oh God,
Cleanse my all.
That I may stand before you,

Unafraid.

12. PRUNING I

Lord, I surrender,
My pride and power to you.

I look inward and see things,
In need of change,
Before your holy presence.

Please change my heart.

I plough up the hard ground,
To receive your seed,
To nurture your seed.

That I may receive the rain,
That I may produce fruit,
For your glory.

13. PRUNING II

Lord, shaping is hard.

My flaws and shortcomings stare me down,
In the past, I would have run away,
To not face my frailty.

But today, I bow my pride and power to you,
I submit to your correction,
I submit to your shaping.

You know the end product you seek,
You know the intensity of the flame required,
To forge this vessel called honour.

At the right time,
You will bring me out,
Of the furnace,
To shine for your glory.

Thank you for loving me,
You gaze at me in a profound way,
You refuse that I rot in mediocrity,
You correct me in love.

I will fulfil your plans for me,
Your plans and purposes,
Are yes and amen in Christ Jesus.

I submit to your Lordship,
And the tools you choose,
To make me the woman,
You've called me to be.

I rely on your strength,

To endure the process,
I am assured you are with me,
Through the seasons,
There is a time,
For everything.

In this time of growth,
I dig my heels firmly,
Into your soil,
I will not be crushed,
By its pressure,
The life within,
Will ooze out.

I will grow to be a mighty oak,
Firmly rooted,
Providing shade,
To the nations.

Thank you for loving me,
Perfectly.
Amen.

14. THE CHOICE BEFORE ME

When I find it hard to forgive,
Please help me, Lord.

I want to forgive,
I choose to forgive,
I will not embrace bitterness,
I know you are working out your plan for my life.

Beyond what has happened,
I choose to trust in you,
I trust your heart for me,
I trust you will take care of me.

Standing securely in this trust,
I release every grievance,
Even when I have been wronged,
I remind my soul,
God is sovereign,
Whatever was meant for evil,
He can turn around for my good.

Lord, I know you are good,
Your love is good,
Teach me to love as you do.

I choose forgiveness and love,
I reject bitterness and rage,
You are sovereign I humble myself before you.

15. THE HURT MIRROR

I am stronger than I realise,
Because you are my strength,
Thank you for who you've made me.

For those I have hurt with my attitude,
Actions and comments,
I pray you heal them.

Whatever hurt exists in me,
Causing me to act in negative ways,
I pray you heal these also.

Tackle the root, Lord,
Restore me to who you called me to be,
I don't want to be the person helping others,
Yet unable to help herself,
Start with me, Lord.

Bring me peace, joy, love, patience,
Trust, gentleness, self-discipline and faith,
Bring me into those things against which there is no law,ᵛ
Help me follow your counsel and walk,
Into the glorious destiny you have for me.

Restore,
Refresh,
Make as new,
Make as you will.

16. IN NEED OF HEALING

Thank you, Jesus,
For who you are to me,
For what you have done in and for me,
For what you are doing now.

Thank you for your healing,
Your restoration, and the path to wholeness.

You saw me, saved me,
Are shepherding me to a glorious future,
Counting on the Lord to prevail,
I take heart and gain strength.[vi]

May the road I travel be filled,
With constant reminders of your faithfulness,
May my heart be soft toward you,
May my life please your heart.

I trust you, Lord, I fix my eyes on you,
My ears await your footsteps,
Be my shepherd, guardian, and guide,[vii]
Lead me in the best pathway for my life.

Faithful God,
Overcome in me,
Overcome for me,
Your kingdom come,
Your will be done.

17. HIS LOVE NEVER QUITS

He heals my broken heart,
His love never quits.

He surrounds me with cords of human kindness,
His love never quits.

He blesses my work, giving me wisdom and courage,
His love never quits.

He helps me stay faithful where I once faltered,
His love never quits.

He provides for my needs,
His love never quits.

He restores my life,
His love never quits.

He restores my hope,
His love never quits.

He corrects me when I am wrong,
His love never quits.

He answers my prayers,
His love never quits.

For journey mercies,
His love never quits.

For favour beyond compare,
His love never quits.

Today, tomorrow, forever,
His love never quits.

18. THE VOICE OF MY PAST

A child learning to walk,
Will fall many times before standing in truth,
With each step she gains strength,
Till what tripped her yesterday has no sway on her steps,
For she has strength and balance against such slights,
With each step, the frequency of falls abate,
Till one day she stands, walks, runs,
She becomes an expert at navigating what once ailed her.

As a child learns to walk,
So I learn to overcome every ail,
There may be stumbles along the way,
But with each passing season,
The frequency of falls must abate,
As I gain strength and balance in the Lord,
The day will come when I stand, walk, run,
A God helped daughter,
Navigating successfully what once ailed me.

Holy Spirit, I know my past,
Created an unconducive environment for you,
I sincerely apologise,
I need you, I cannot do this without you,
The ability to overcome comes from you.

Please do not give up on me,
Help me not feed what ails me,
But instead, eat onto wholeness,
Please help Lord.

19. FORGIVE YOURSELF

How can God be reaching out his hand and I ignore it?

It seems like pride,
Preposterous even,
I come to his throne,
Head bowed,
Expecting a rebuke.

I avoid his throne,
Avoiding the scorn expected in his eyes,
He sends messengers out,
Go find her he commands,
Go bring her in,
She has been out too long,
She must be catching a cold,
I miss her,
I want to see her face,
I long to see her face.

Instead of scorn,
I see eyes filled with mercy,
Eyes telling me all is forgiven.

Don't live there anymore, daughter,
No one felt what you went through than I,
No one deserves to feel hurt than I,
But I have chosen to forget it,
I say to you, all is forgiven.

Don't you feel my love all around you?

I am not dwelling on the past,
Stop sitting there, I am moving forward,
Doing a new thing,viii
I need you to do the same,
Choose to move on,
That's my girl!
That's it.

Worry not about the process,
I am holding you,
I will help you,
Remember, you are very precious to me.

Precious things are treated as precious,
They are kept securely and shined regularly,
They embody the love,
Of the one who made them precious.

20. THE LURKING SHADOW

Pride, the lurking shadow.

Absent in some areas of life yet magnificently present in others,
Pride, relying on my strength instead of your ability,
Pride, declaring I will never do 'such and such',
Rather than realising, you enable me to do right.

This lurking shadow is one not easily seen,
So I thank you for illuminating my soul,
With light so bright I can see.

You are merciful,
You are patient,
I am humbled,
I am grateful.

You are the source of my strength,
The source of all I am,
The source of all I have.

For every proud thought, action, and word,
I repent, Lord, please forgive me and make me whole,
It is by your grace alone I stand,
Restore me to yourself,
Like only you can.

21. WEIGHTS

The weight of the season,
Heavy on my shoulders,
No physical help to ease the strain,
I can't see my way out.

God, you are my God.

Your help is available to me,
Please send me help,
Directly from your throne.

God, you are my God.

I receive what you send, in Jesus' name,
You remain worthy of my trust,
I will not be overwhelmed.

God, you are my God.

22. THE NAVIGATOR

Navigating this sea is not my strong suit,
I know you who formed the seas,
And plotted their route,
Please lead me though.

Societal conditioning in me,
But contrary to you,
Please highlight and uproot.

Fear conditioning in me,
Is contrary to you,
Please highlight and uproot.

Pride conditioning in me
Is contrary to you,
Please highlight and uproot.

Environmental conditioning in me,
But contrary to you,
Please highlight and uproot.

Experiential conditioning in me,
But contrary to you,
Please highlight and uproot.

I trust you, Lord.

23. THE LONG WALK HOME

I chased a pot of solid gold,
To the bow of the rain, I chased,
But all I saw was glittering dust,
And vanity it was.

'Cos when I turned to chase the gold,
I turned my back on you,
You who my gem and treasure is,
My very heart, my all.

Now turning back I look to you,
Illuminate my soul,
With light so bright,
I clearly see,
My way back home to you.

SEUN OMOHA

Seasons of Failing Strength

I sow seeds of prayer into God's garden,
that they may grow and yield a godly
harvest.

24. FLOURISHING

A piece of land flourishes,
By a combination of factors,
Seed, soil, water, and sun.

I pray the seed you planted in me will not wither,
Right seeds produce the right fruits and trees,
Trees of God's planting,
For the display of his splendour.[ix]

I pray for the right soil in my heart,
Good soil conducive for your seed,
Supplements and additives chosen by you,
So everything works together for good.

I pray for the water, yes,
It is possible to depend on irrigation systems,
Man-made interventions,
But that is a sign of drought,
A sign of planting out-of-season,
Lord, this is your season,
I pray against the drought,
I ask for rain in the time of rain,
That every field becomes a lush paradise.[x]

I pray for the sun,
Your glorious presence,
To yield a land of flourishing,
By your grace.

25. BEAUTIFUL YOU

Be not so enamoured by beauty,
That you forget character.

The face you wear,
Is what people see.

Who you are inside,
Is the person they meet.

26. GROWING... BLOOMING

Words of others, though important,
Whether positive or negative,
Should not colour the view of God's gift.

I want to be grounded in God,
Knowing who I am in him,
Being true to what he has placed in my hands.

When positive words come,
They should be accepted with gratitude,
Gratitude to their source,
And to God, who the glory belongs to,
Such words should never become an idol,
For which I bend backwards to elicit same again,
Everything must be in its place,
I must be true to who I am.

When criticism comes,
I must not be quick to defend myself,
Glean the good, use that to grow,
Throw away the chaff,
See it not as an attack on your person,
God corrects those he loves,
Listen, make the necessary adjustments,
Everything must be in its place,
I must be true to who I am.

Who I am called to be in God.

27. YOU ARE VALUABLE

Daughter,
Know your value and worth in me,
I made you beautiful,
I made you priceless,
I made you unique,
I made it so specifically.

It pleased me to make you,
Do not despise who you are,
I love all of you,
Remember that,
As you navigate the seasons.

When I decide to bring about fulfilment in certain areas,
I send people specifically to shape that area of your life,
But in all remember,
I am the one, who knows the product,
I seek to achieve.

I am pleased with you,
It pleases me to see you long for me,
Longing for godliness,
Longing to be whole,
I am the one who fulfils your longing,
Cling to me!

I love you, darling, warts and all,
I'll treat your warts out of my love.

Balance, I will teach,
Desires, I will give,
Weakness, I will strengthen.

I will polish the brass,
Shine the silver,
Display the gold,
I will make you,
Who I have created you to be.

I am not done with you,
I have only begun,
Keep your eyes on me, my girl,
I will lead you safely home.

28. WORDS. LIFE. LOVE

You affirm me in the depths of my soul,
You cause life to blossom.

You stoop down and whisper sweet words in my ears,
You cause life to blossom.

Your words awaken courage in me,
They kindle life within me.

Your words give me the strength to climb the next mountain,
That I may stand facing their source.

Your words are a fragrant offering,
Refreshing the core of my being.

Words are important,
Yes, words are important,
I know yours come from a place of love,
A place of love beyond compare.

Words. Life. Love

29. I AM YOURS

Lead me, Holy Spirit.

Help me see as you see,
Help me trust you without limit,
Let your perfect love cast out every fear.

Thank you for your work in me,
I am not my own, I am yours,
Let your peace rule my heart,
I cannot make things happen for my sake,
I trust you to make them happen for me.

Let my eyes not turn away from your face, my Lord,
Help me be balanced in what I do,
To find balance in how I do it,
Come have your way in me,
Break away things that are not of you,
Give me focus.

Let me not raise an idol before you,
The throne of my heart is yours alone,
And out of your Lordship of my life,
I will live purposeful and effective,
An excellent life,
For your glory.

30. JUST ENOUGH LIGHT

In the life of faith, sometimes you see nothing more than the next step,
God gives just enough light for the very next step,
Whilst all around, darkness surrounds.

The heart filled with faith plods on through the darkness,
Knowing that underneath are the everlasting arms,[xi]
And the path crafted by God will lead to a destination,
Better than it could have asked or hoped for.

Your faith challenge, daughter, is to trust me,
Even when you don't understand,
When you can't think it through,
When you can't see how, why, when or where,
Trust that I have the best-laid plans for you,
Leading you to a glorious destiny.

You may not understand, but I do,
Trust me through the season,
Indeed, I am your place of refuge,[xii]
A refuge of rest for all that you are,
Your mind, body, and life in every sphere,
I am in control, I am in charge, I am pleased with you,
I will lead you as I purpose.

Sitting in the centre of your love and presence,
I bow my desire to your purpose,
I trust you, lead me step by step.

31. YOU ARE GOOD

Irrespective of what you do,
Or don't in my life,
The fact remains,
That you are God and you are good.

You deserve all my worship,
And I give it to you today,
Be glorified, Daddy.

Above all,
In my life,
Be exalted,
Be fully praised.

May your name,
Be lifted high,
For there indeed,
Is nobody like you.

32. THE UNKNOWN WILDERNESS

Some days we walk,
Through the wilderness,
Without knowing.

We feel our soles tire,
We feel our soul tire,
We see our arms weaken,
We see our faith falter.

Yet, it never occurs to us,
That what we walk through,
Is nothing, but a wilderness.

It is not that we have no strength,
But that we must learn,
Reliance on our strength,
Is futility itself.

So, with each step,
Through the wilderness,
Our strength is battered,
By storm clouds, sandstorms, and hail.

We wonder why God,
Would let us walk through hell,
We doubt his love,
And his ability to save.

Yet he says,
Only by breaking you,
Can I make you reflect me,
As I want to be seen.

Unknown to us we walked each mile,

Through the wilderness,
Then a faint glimpse,
Catches our eyes.

We see before us a picture of calm,
Could it be?
A season of rest, before me awaits?
A change to my circumstances exists?

At the threshold a smiling father awaits,
You held on, my darling,
You walked through the fire to get to me,
Now enter the season of rest.

Here before you lie,
All you strived for in the wilderness,
For there I taught you to wait,
But now I give you to freely to enjoy.

O that we may recognise,
The wilderness for what it is,
For then we shall see,
It is nothing but a gateway to God.

33. COURAGE

The one who calls me,
To be strong and courageous,
Does so without regard for my capacity,
But that I may avail myself,
Of his strength and courage,
Which is ever present for me.

34. BY YOUR POWER

I am resisting your will,
I repent.

I am willing to be made willing,
Help me recognise and want,
What you want for me.

Back to this bad attitude cycle again,
I see pride, anger, grumbling,
Complaining, gossip and ingratitude.

All these sins, I confess to you,
Please forgive and cleanse me,
From the hidden sins in my heart.

By your power I am strong,
By your wisdom I am wise,
By your mercy I have grace,
By your will I have courage.

I lay down my ideas,
And receive your best for me.

Thank you for hearing me,
My powerful God.

35. A CRY FOR HELP

Lord, I am bruised.

I am drained, emotionally distressed,
Crying buckets,
Angry in bursts,
Sad in waves, tired, exhausted.

Lord, come in,
Please help me.

Let your joy be my strength,[xiii]
Come into this season of my life.

Come in your glory,
In your strength and power,
In your goodness and wisdom.

I need your help,
Lord, please help me.

36. WHEN TEARS ABOUND

Lord Jesus, I thank you.

When all is said and done,
The chips are down,
The storm rages,
My strength is weak,
And tears abound.

Yet my soul knows,
The blessed consolation,
Of strength and encouragement,
That comes through your word.

When my strength fails,
I find my strength in you,
When my heart fails,
I find that you are stronger,
Than my heart and you know all.

When tears abound,
I find you to be my joy,
A shoulder to bear all,
You are my dearest father,
Dependable and trustworthy,
The king of my heart, my salvation.

Today I come before you, saying thank you,
Amid my tears,
Because I know,
Overriding all this is your sovereignty,
My assurance you are in control.

You are working all things,

To their farthest good,
For your great glory,
My tears are not a surprise to you,
I know the road to be travelled,
Is not hidden from your face.

Holy Spirit, encourage my heart with your word,
Teach me the next step to take,
I depend solely on your guidance,
For the way forward,
Your one action solves many things,
I know you are all-powerful.

Through this season,
I remind myself of your sovereignty and purpose,
I ask for the grace to trust,
And follow after you each day,
Victory is mine in you.

Amen.

37. I DECIDE

Today was a hard day,
Stresses and pressures all around.

Lord in my strength,
I cannot live the life you've called me to,
I need your help through this season,
And the seasons ahead.

I decide I am going to push past the strain,
I decide I will succeed,
I decide I can do all things,
Through Christ who strengthens me.[xiv]

38. A VESSEL CALLED HONOUR

Challenge me not,
She cried from within,
I am but a little vase.

Looking at her,
The potter replies,
The challenge I give,
Will ply you with strength.

Challenge me not,
Oh, challenge me not,
My frame is weak,
My heart is a fragile thing.

I know your frame,
I know your strength,
I know what you'll become,
Only rely on my love.

The potter with love,
Puts the vase in the furnace,
And with each passing minute,
She awakens to truth,
That her resilience,
Is more than she ever knew.

Just in time,
Doors swing wide,
Vase and Potter reunite.

A new lease on life,
A strength beyond compare,
A vessel called Honour,
Whose journey has just begun.

Seasons of Hope

Traces of God have the ability to rekindle the torch of hope in the coldest of hearts.

39. THE LEARNER

I will learn what is pleasing to the Lord,
I will apply these to my life,
I will reflect on my walk,
As I aim to live a life,
That constantly shows,
What is most acceptable to God.[xv]

So help me God.

40. JOY IN PURPOSE

The eyes of the Lord are set to do you good.

Since I've determined to do you good,
Sit back and watch me show off with your life.
My purposes towards you are of good and not of evil,
I have a plan,
I have a purpose.

Every desire you have,
Is laid plain before my face,
And now I am ready to work on them one by one.

Your character I will shape and mould,
For I want you to reflect the real me,
Not who you think I am.

Peace like a river I speak to you,
I banish fear.
Love unrestrained I pour once again,
Into the core of who you are.

Your life will once again be filled with joy,
Every fruit of my Spirit will be worked in you,
As you have desired.

I stand ready to do all this,
And yes! It shall be done.

41. PHOENIX

Yesterday is past, yesterday is gone.

As the early morning dew disperses at the rising of the sun,
So yesterday is at the dawn of today,
Yesterday, with its successes and failures,
Yesterday, with its heartbreak and tears,
Yesterday, with its dancing and joy,
All gone like the rising vapour.

Glimpses of yesterday in the recess of my mind,
Show a door firmly locked,
If only I could return and relive some of it,
If only I could enjoy the successes again,
If only I could avoid the failures again,
If only I could do it all over,
That, my dear, is an effort in futility,
For indeed yesterday is past, gone, sealed shut.

O daughter,
Rise from the ashes of yesterday,
Rise like the phoenix from the flame,
Burn bright today,
Blaze into tomorrow.

All learned from numerous yesterdays,
Have shaped today,
Like a woman carefully picking,
The bean seed from its husk,
Choose food from the husk of yesterday,
To sustain today and,
Give strength for tomorrow,
You know not what lies ahead,

Yet you know the one who holds the keys.

The sun rises,
It grows brighter,
Unto the noonday,[xvi]
So shall my path be,
As this phoenix rises,
Into her today.

42. PRESSING IN

The making of a woman,
Is mine to accomplish,
And that I will,
As you press into me.

The days seem long,
But the end is in sight,
I will fulfil all I have set out to do.

Lord, you are awesome,
Wonderful, faithful,
Kind, generous,
You are my King.

My friend, burden bearer,
Biggest encourager,
Lover of my soul,
My peace.

I honour and thank you,
I love and adore you,
I praise you,
I lift you high.

Let my faith break through,
The walls of my heart,
Into my hands and feet,
Let what I believe move me to action.

43. REVOLUTIONS

My Story and God's story,
How very different.

My story was,
Married at 25, kids at 27,
My story revolved around stages of life,
The next step to be attained.

God's story was,
Singapore at 26, Seoul at 28,
God's story revolved around his plan,
The best step to be attained.

I pray my story,
Will always be swallowed,
By God's story for me.

That my every day will be lived out in detail,
According to your plan for my life.

This journey has just begun,
For this vessel called honour.

44. HAVING DONE ALL, STAND

You did not lead me to the bank of the sea,
To be overcome by it.

Fear behind,
Scepticism around,
Sea before,
All hold no weight in your sight.

My strength comes from above,
Looking up I see YOU,
Seated in glory,
Poised as a warrior ready to act.

You have not brought me here,
To be overwhelmed,
No! But to experience another dimension,
Of who you are.

The God of all flesh,
To whom nothing is impossible,
To whom nothing is difficult.

The dawning of the sun today,
Reveals the glory of the Lord,
Making a way through the sea,
Leading me on dry ground,
To his promised land.

So, with assurance,
I face the sea again,
There is only one way, FORWARD!
Fear and scepticism have had their day.
Having done all, I stand.

45. RUTH'S PRAYER, MY PRAYER

I have pitched my tent in the land of hope,
I have pitched my tent in the land of truth,
Forgetting the things which are behind,
I lay hold of what is ahead,
For great is what is to come.

I will go about my daily business,
Doing what my hands find to do with excellence,
I know every step leads to a place of hope,
I know every step is leading home.

I have pitched my tent in the land of hope,
I will not be disappointed.

46. HIM, ME AND THE MOUNTAIN

Standing before this mountain,
I quiver in fear,
I've been here before, defeated before,
I tried my very best,
Mustered all the courage I had,
Stood my ground,
But, the mountain laughed me to scorn,
In shame, defeated, I retreated.

Here I am again, before the same old mountain,
I hear the laugh, I hear the taunts,
But this time, something is different,
This time I know I can make it.

My eyes drift from the mountain to the footsteps beside me,
I look around me and see
The presence of Him who made the mountains,
He points, I follow and see before me
Angels at the foot of the mountain.

Suddenly! There is silence,
The mountain is silent,
The mountain fears as now I know greater is He with me,
I shout "Who are you O mountain before me?
You shall become a levelled ground",[xvii]
I look at my father,
He smiles His approval,
Again, the silence.

"Proceed!" my father says,
"Proceed my child!"

With shaking feet, I start to move,
Down a path I have walked many a time,

The mountain still stands,
The distance gets shorter,
The mountain still stands.

And then, I hear the sound of many waters,
The voice of the Lord thunders,[xviii]
I see the mountain tremble,
I see the angels create a path for me,
I see the father cheering me on.

And so with confidence, I walk on,
Through the rubble of the once giant mountain,
Crossing to the other side,
I made it because God is with me.

47. THE GOOD SHEPHERD

I am the good shepherd,
The good shepherd lays down his life for his sheep,[xix]
I already laid down my life for you,
How much more will I give you all things,
In accordance with my will.

Come into my love, daughter,
Come and bask in the glory of my love,
Worry not about tomorrow,
I hold tomorrow,
And your tomorrow is bright.

This has been a strange season, I know,
But trust me, I waste nothing,
Every strand of every experience is woven,
Into the beautiful tapestry that is your life.

Fix your eyes on me,
Trust me to lead you through this season,
I am your good shepherd,
Leading you into a good land.

The lines are falling in pleasant places before your feet,[xx]
Sit back and watch me work,
Hitherto I have done nothing,
Now it begins.

48. EAUX VIVANTES

The fountain of living waters that never runs dry,
Christ, my lover, my King, my father, is that living water,
He is the only one that can satisfy my thirst.[xxi]

He touches me where no one else can,
He meets me where I am,
And sees me as I am,
But chooses never to leave me just as I'm found.

He knows when I smile with a hint of sadness,
And knows when I rejoice in truth,
He sees right through my walls,
To the little girl within the shell.

You satisfy me, Lord,
Help me fill myself with you,
And find my rest in you,
Fill me with your Spirit,
That I may never thirst again.

Christ la fontaine d'eau vive.

Seasons of Service

A flower crushed releases the aroma
within.

49. A LIFE LESS ORDINARY

You are calling me to a life less ordinary,
A life with rules different from the norm.

Help me live not by the world's standards,
Nor by the expectations of others,
Help me live instead by your rules.

For if I truly accept as you've made me,
If I choose to be a vessel unto your honour,
If I choose to be joyful in it,
I will reap the rewards.

A life fulfilled.

50. SINK OR SWIM

O Lord,
Help me yield to you.

Like one learning to swim,
The fear of sinking,
Makes the would-be swimmer flap around,
Overextending themselves,
Using every strength and muscle to stay afloat,
Many-a-time such a swimmer becomes exhausted.

Yet there is a better way,
The way of trust,
The way of the seasoned swimmer,
Who has come to know that stillness reveals,
Buoyancy to rise to the surface of the water.

In this perfect stillness,
The water becomes an ally,
Not a foe to beat into submission,
The swimmer floats in unison with the waves,
Yielding to the water's will,
Expending minimal effort.

In my default position,
I am that first swimmer,
Trying to stay afloat,
To balance it all,
To be who I ought.

This constant state of trying,
Has led to exhaustion,
And a realisation there has to be a better way.

Now I hear you say, **YIELD!**

Lord, I want to yield to your Spirit,
As you lead me safely,
Through this journey of life.
Please help me, Lord,

Amen.

51. HE LEADS ME

Now I stand to do all I promised.

A humble heart I seek,
A humble heart I desire,
That which I promised to do,
Unfailingly shall be done.

Indeed, I am great,
I sustain all by the words of my power,[xxii]
Know me, keep your eyes on my face,
Walk with me, those I lead never go astray.

Lean into me, worship me,
I charted the course of your life,
As you lean into me,
I will lead you safely through,
Each season of your days.

Don't pull back,
Love me passionately,
I love you even more.

52. SUBMISSION

Lord, I submit to you.

I am the clay,
You are the potter,[xxiii]
It is you who shapes each vessel,
For the use you intend.

Each scrape, splash, oil, wait,
Knead, reshape, break, Is for a purpose,
For you are a master craftsman,
You know just what is required.

As the clay in your workshop,
I submit to you,
And the process you intend for me,
Till I am ready.

Mould and shape me,
Into that vessel called honour,
For your glory.

You are my shield,
My protection and guide,
My God in whom I trust,
My God who helps me be great,
My God who arms me with strength,
And makes my way perfect,[xxiv]
The one who planned every day of my life,
Before a single day was lived.[xxv]

You are my King,
I submit to your will.

Bring clarity,
Bring peace,
I love you with all my heart.

53. THE MASTER'S CALL

Be still my beating,
Wondering heart,
To hear your Master's call.

He sits enthroned,
On highest heights,
And reaches down,
To earth.

My soul he seeks,
And longs to reach,
My hand to take and guide.

The path he's laid,
Before my feet,
To teach me,
To apply.

So be thou still,
My beating heart,
To hear,
Your master's call.

54. SEEDS OF GODLINESS

There are depths,
And heights in you Lord,
There is more to grow into.

There is here and now,
And beyond, completeness of maturity,
In godliness of mind and character.

Lord, from where I am today,
I seek your mercy,
Help me grow in you,
Water the seeds of godliness in me.

Remove the things,
Old or new,
Which have been choking out,
Your seed in me.

Show me your mercy,
I ask in Jesus' name,
Amen.

55. DEALING WITH THE PAST

Lord, take me deeper.

Past the gates and failures of my past,
Repeated stumbling blocks,
That land me facedown,
Time and again.

You stand at the door and knock,[xxvi]
With tired feet and hands,
I approach the door,
I open up to you, Lord.

Come into secret places,
Failures secretly cherished,
Places I hid,
From the glare of your holiness.

Come in with the fire of your presence,
Cleanse me,
That I may follow you,
To the terrain only the holy tread.

Douse me with oil,
Sustain the flame you began,
Let your oil flow,
Into every part of me,
Fill me up, Lord,
Help me submit to you even more.

56. TRACES OF GOD

Creator God knows his creation perfectly,
He knows what catches our eye,
He knows our passions,
He knows what stimulates our intellect,
He knows how to catch our attention.

He is the perfect suitor,
He does not bombard you,
Until you love him, No.

He throws out a bone,
And waits for the scent,
Or sight, as in the case of Moses,
To turn our head to see,
Then He calls out.

Traces of God.

I wonder how many times,
God has tried to turn my head to see,
But I paid him no attention.

I wonder how many times,
I have been drawn to what he did,
But dismissed God, the doer,
I recognised the gift,
But ignored God, the giver.

I wonder how many times,
My heart beat faster,
As I recognised the trace God left me,
I turned aside to see,
But ignored the call that followed.

I pray, like Moses, when the call comes,
I will have the boldness to respond,
Here I am.

I pray, like Moses, I will recognise,
The traces of God in my life.

I pray I will not despise,
Abuse or ignore,
The trace, the call.

But gratefully recognise,
The voice of the doer,
In the midst of the flame.

For every gift is to proclaim,
The presence of the giver,
The one who calls me by name.

57. DISTRACTIONS

Lord, my heart gets distracted,
Please help me.

In trying to maintain,
Or fulfil a reputation,
In longing for wealth and riches,
In placing desires above you.

Help my heart,
Yearn for you above all else.

Let my character,
Be more important than my reputation.

Let purpose outweigh,
The glitz and glamour of wealth.

Let your will override,
The draw of desire.
Let my heart fix its gaze on you.

58. IDOLS

Lord I pray, I will not raise,
What you bless me with,
As an idol before you.

Thank you for writing my story,
As it unfolds page by page,
Help me have the patience,
To live each scene.

Help me trust you for the grand finale,
I love you with all my heart.

59. A RAINY DAY

Lord, in this season, enlist me into your purpose.
In this season, when the windows of heaven are open,
Let your rain fall on every field of my life,
To become a lush and fruitful pasture.[xxvii]

In the field of my work,
Let your rain fall.

In the field of my mind,
Heart, thoughts, wisdom,
Let your rain fall.

Help me be at peace,
For you have said you will provide,
And you stand ready to.

In the field of my dreams,
Hopes, purpose, hobbies and aspirations,
Let your rain fall.

Let my life grow,
From the mire and opposition of the past,
Into the life you want it to be.

Let your rain soak me thoroughly.
I agree with your Spirit,
I say Amen.

60. THE CRUSHING

Lord, you formed me.

You sent me to my family,
To the nation of my birth,
To the cities of my dwelling.

Every detail of my life,
Has been orchestrated,
And permitted by you,
Leading me to today.

I pray that crushing experiences,
Of my life will release the aroma,
You placed within me.

The flies that seek to spoil the ointment,
I pray you'll remove,
Only by laying myself before you,
Will I become who you want me to be.

Where I stood in my strength,
Woman and proud,
I humble myself before you.

Let me not die,
Carrying the aroma, untouched,
The aroma you wanted me,
To share with my world.

That I miss not the purpose,
For which I was created.

When the bus of destiny pulls up,
Help me not be distracted by other things,

That I miss the main thing.

Help me never to hold,
The things in my current focus,
Higher than you,
And your purpose for me.

Guide me, Lord,
On the things I can and should do,
Help me not procrastinate,
Help me not be lazy.

Let my ears be ever more,
Attentive to your voice,
You promised to shepherd me,
Help me be an obedient sheep.

As you teach, help me learn,
As you lead, help me follow.

61. THE STILL VOICE

In the stillness, In the quiet,
I hear your voice,
That casts out every fear.

Your voice gives me courage,
To step out of the boat and,
Experience what it is to walk on water.

In the stillness,
My spirit awakens, and my soul sings.

In the stillness,
I find you, I find myself.

In the stillness,
I am reminded of the truth,
Of your sovereignty,
Of you, the source of my life.

Lord, I am here,
I have turned to see,
I know you are present to meet with me,
Help me be open to receiving from you.

You are a God who speaks,
Do not keep silent over me,
Speak that which you know I need to hear,
Speak that which will lead me,
Along the best pathways for my life.[xxviii]

Assure me of your will,
That I will be the woman,
You have called me to be,
Today and tomorrow.

In the stillness, In the quiet.

62. THE GOOD FRIEND

Lord, I pray about my attitude to life,
And I speak to my soul, these truths.

Be not self-serving,
Seek not the praise of men,
Seek God's approval in all you do.

Be not prideful,
Believing your press,
Acknowledge God, in all, as your source.

Face your future,
Do what your hands find to do,
With excellence, for God's glory.

Humble your heart before God,
As he takes you higher,
Keep your eyes on him.

Be generous with what you have been given,
Be a good friend,
Honour God, honour men,
Be true, honest, and loving.

Where maturity is needed,
Grow and develop,
Ultimately I pray, to shine for his glory.

63. GIVING MY BEST

You deserve more than I can give,
Yet I desire to give you my very best.

My best when I wake up each day,
My best when I relate with my neighbours,
My best when I catch up with my friends,
My best when I make plans,
My best when I work,
My best when I serve.

I love you, Lord,
You warm the cockles of my heart.

Seasons of Change

As you teach I will learn, I will follow as you lead.

64. PEACE IN THE STORM

Lord, I thank you for peace,
Another season of upheaval,
But I am at peace.

I know you are sovereign,
I know you will use this new season,
To propel me towards the shores,
Of the next stage of my life.

I lean in,
I press my ears to your heart,
I humble my will,
To follow as you lead.

65. PROMISE KEEPER

You are my light,
You lead me,
You are my hope,
You strengthen me.

You lead me on,
Through sacred places,
You lead me on,
Into your promise.

I walk on the path,
You show me,
I trust in you, Lord,
With everything.

I will not fear,
The stormy waters,
You lead me on,
Into your promise.

You're the promise keeper,
I know you are,
You hold the world,
In the hollow of your hand.
You're my promise keeper,
You will lead me, Into your promise.

66. ANXIOUS THOUGHTS

The lack of peace in my heart,
The anxiety I feel,
Is a true testament to,
My lack of trust in you.

It is a testament to,
My trying to control,
What is yours to handle.

I have neither strength nor wisdom,
To handle this season,
Yet I try to do the impossible,
This is a futile endeavour.

Today, Lord,
I relinquish the control,
I hold on my future,
I hand it over to you.

The desires I strive to meet,
 Only you can fulfil,
Only you can give me peace.

I release my grasp,
Fill my life with your perfect peace,
And teach me to trust you.

67. A NEW YEAR

In this new year, Lord,
I pray for clarity of purpose and direction,
I pray for accelerated restoration,
Let wasted years be recovered and surpassed.

I pray for the courage to trust in you,
Wholehearted trust moving me,
In the direction you lead.

I pray for grace to flourish,
Let everything in my hands blossom,
Cause doors to swing wide for me,
Do a new thing, Lord,[xxix]
Let my eyes see it,
I know what you begin, you will complete.

Go on this journey with me,
Do mighty things, give great gifts,
I give you my heart once again,
Come take your place on its throne,
And be glorified through me.

Shepherd me, Lord,
Prune me, give me a new lease on life,
And joy beyond compare,
Make me a woman of substance,
A woman of excellence and integrity,
Living for the glory of your name.

68. A NEW SEASON

Lord, in this new season,
I speak your purpose over every second.

I speak your life into my heart,
Your life into my health,
Your life into my family,
Your life into my relationships.

I speak your perfect will over all my hands find to do,
Your peace over all that concerns me,
Your peace and your will over my nation.

I pray every field of my life,
Becomes a lush paradise by your grace,[xxx]
I pray for grace to sit at your feet,
And learn from you.

Guide me, Lord,
Teach me, lead me,
Into treasures that delight my being.

I pray for peace on every side,
I surmount the struggles of past seasons,
I will not fight the same battles,
The Lord will give me victory,
He will fight for me, and I will hold my peace.[xxxi]

I pray for every new endeavour,
That the Lord will be right in the centre,
Reveal your will and your pleasure in each endeavour.

I pray for the courage to do the right thing,
To take the risks necessary for progress,
To live unlimited and jump into the great things,

You have planned for me.

I pray for accelerated progress in every sphere of life,
I call forth the seed of greatness within me,
Let the seed become an oak of righteousness,
That will provide shade to many.

I pray for grace to be open,
And honest in my walk with you,
I pray to receive more of your love,
I pray for authenticity in my dealings.

Let joy overflow my life,
Let joy radiate from me.

I will be confident in my portion in you,
Make much of your name in my life.

69. HOPE IN THE STORM

I am not as those without help,
Those grappling in the dark for anything to hold to.

I am not as those without hope,
Without assurance of a future.

I am not as those with confusing thoughts,
Who act out of necessity unsure of a good outcome.

I am a daughter of the King of kings,
The Lord of lords, master of the universe,
All-knowing God.

I am a princess of the King,
All he has is available to me,
For he is my father.

As death could not hold him down,
So may he not be caged in my life,
May God accomplish all his will,
To the glory of his name.

My hope is in God,
My strength and wisdom are from God,
My knowledge is from God,
I have a joyous future in God.

70. PRECIOUS STONES

In my relationship with you,
I admit I have conditional modifiers.

If God loves me,
He would have given me my desire,
He would have given me a stress-free life,
He would have provided for my needs.

Lord, I hear you loud and clear,
It has to be you plus nothing,
My relationship with you,
Should have no conditional modifiers.

You are more than enough,
You are worthy of my love,
You are a good father, all-powerful,
Able to do what you will without resistance.

I lay at your feet,
The precious stones I carry close to my heart,
These distractions from your face,
I lay before you.

Help me love you truly,
Not through the glass of my desires,
I hunger and thirst for your righteousness,[xxxii]
Expressed in and through me,
For the glory of your name.

These precious stones I open to you,
Do what you will,
Your perfect will.

So let it be Lord,
Amen.

SEUN OMOHA

The Spirit Walk on Emotions Avenue

Our emotions can appear all-consuming when we focus on them and the feelings they awaken in us. Yet if we are to truly live the abundant life God promises, we must learn to:

- Yield to the Holy Spirit for his guidance and power,

- Enforce the reality of God's word over our circumstances, and

- Abandon the cravings of our self-life.

Whatever the prevailing emotion of your current season, you are sure to find succour for your soul in the place of communion with your Heavenly Father.

I make bold to say, dear sister, that you too can encourage yourself in the Lord your God.

Galatians 5:16:

> *So I say, let the Holy Spirit guide your lives. Then you won't be doing what your sinful nature craves. (NLT)*

> *Let me emphasise this: As you yield to the dynamic life and power of the Holy Spirit, you will abandon the cravings of your self-life. (TPT)*

1 Samuel 30:6:

> *…but David strengthened himself in the Lord his God. (ESV)*

When you are...	Remember...	Scripture Says...	Letters from LOVE...
Angry, Bitter	Bitter waters can become sweet	Ephesians 4:31-32 Exodus 15:23-25	14, 34, 35, 54
Anticipating	His hope does not disappoint	Romans 5:5	5, 6, 24, 31, 43, 67, 68, 70
Anxious	His peace To trust in God	Philippians 4:6-7	22, 29, 47, 53, 59, 64, 66
Defeated, Resigned to fate	To surrender to His will	Jeremiah 29:11	13, 26, 39, 49, 52, 56
Discouraged	To wait upon the Lord	Isaiah 40:29-31	28, 48, 65, 69
Envious	His Faithfulness Godliness with contentment is great gain	1 Thessalonians 5:24 2 Timothy 2:13	4, 7, 8, 42
Exhausted, Stressed	A bruised reed He will not break He will give rest	Isaiah 42:3 Matthew 11:28	21, 28, 32, 35, 37, 38, 50
Fearful	The just shall live by faith	Hebrews 10:38 Isaiah 41:10	3, 28, 30, 33, 44, 46, 61
Joyful, Optimistic	His goodness To be grateful	Psalm 31:19	1, 2, 58, 63
Prideful	He gives grace to the Humble	James 4:6 1 Peter 5:6	12, 20, 34, 51, 57, 60, 62
Remorseful	He delights to show mercy	Hebrews 4:16 Lamentations 3:22-23	9, 10, 11, 15, 18, 19, 23, 55
Sad, Hurt	His Joy is strength	Nehemiah 8:10 Isaiah 12:3	16, 17, 35, 36
Uncertain about the future	His love is everlasting	Jeremiah 31:3	25, 27, 40, 41, 45

notes

Precious things embody the love of the one who made them precious.

My Letter From Love

Now that you have read Her Father's Daughter: Letters From Love, why not write your letter from love to your Father?

References

i Proverbs 13:12
ii Psalm 121:4
iiiMatthew 5: 8
iv Psalm 51: 10-12
v Galatians 5: 23
vi Habakkuk 3:19
vii Psalm 32:8
viii Isaiah 43: 18-19
ix Isaiah 61: 3
x Zechariah 10: 1
xi Deuteronomy 33: 27
xii Psalm 91: 1
xiii Nehemiah 8: 10
xiv Philippians 4: 13
xv Ephesians 5: 10 (AMP)
xvi Proverbs 4: 18
xvii Zechariah 4: 7
xviii Psalm 29: 3
xix John 10:11
xx Psalm 16: 6
xxi John 4: 14
xxii Hebrews 1: 3
xxiii Jeremiah 18:2-6
xxiv Psalm 18: 32
xxv Psalm 138: 16
xxvi Revelations 3: 20
xxvii Zechariah 10: 1 (NLT)
xxviii Psalm 32: 8 (NLT)
xxix Isaiah 43: 19
xxx Zechariah 10:1; Isaiah 32: 15
xxxi Exodus 4: 14
xxxii Matthew 5: 6

Printed in Great Britain
by Amazon

57616922R00067